Science Around Us
Pull and Push

Sally Hewitt

Chrysalis Children's Books

First published in the UK in 2003 by
Chrysalis Children's Books
An imprint of Chrysalis Books Group Plc
The Chrysalis Building, Bramley Road
London W10 6SP

Paperback edition first published in 2005
Copyright © Chrysalis Books Group Plc 2003

ISBN 1 84138 717 7 (hb)
ISBN 1 84458 276 0 (pb)

British Library Cataloguing in Publication Data
for this book is available from the British Library.

Editorial manager: Joyce Bentley
Project editor: Clare Weaver
Designer: Wladek Szechter
Picture researcher: Aline Morley
Consultant: Helen Walters

Printed in China
10 9 8 7 6 5 4 3 2 1

Words in **bold** can be found in Words to remember on page 30.

Picture credits
Cover ; Jon P. Yeager/Corbis
Insets (L-R); Derke/O'Hara/Getty, Colin Garratt; Milepost 92 _/ Corbis, Loisjoy Thuston/Bubbles, Brownie Harris/Corbis ; Back cover ; Shona Wood/Bubbles ©Bubbles P5 Bruno Zarri, P6 Loisjoy Thurston, P9 (T) David Robinson, P14 Chris Rout, P15 Chris Rout, P16 Jennie Woodcock, P17 Loisjoy Thurston, P18 Shona Wood, P24 Loisjoy Thurston, ©Corbis P1 Colin Garratt/ Milepost 92 _, P7 Colin Garratt/Milepost 92 _, P8 Jon P.Yeager, P9 E H Wallop, P12 Museum of Flight, P13 Amos Nachoum, P19 Michael S Yamashita, P20 Anthony Nex , P21 Steve Lupton, P23 (T) Royalty-Free,(B) Michael St. Maur Sheil, P25 Ed Bock, P26 Brownie Harris, P27 David Pu'u ©Getty P4 Peter Correz, P10 Derke/O'Hara, P11 Lori Adamski Peek, P22 Ray Massey

Contents

Pull and push   4

Moving along   6

Stop and change direction   8

Friction   10

Moving through air and water   12

Twist and turn   14

Squash and stretch   16

Falling down   18

Heavy and light   20

Floating and sinking   22

Magnets   24

Wind and waves   26

Make a parachute   28

Words to remember   30

Index   32

Pull and push

Things move because something or someone gives them a pull or a push. Pushes and pulls are kinds of **forces** that make things move.

You pull on your socks and your football boots.

When you kick a football, you give it a strong push with your foot.

Your **muscles** pull the **bones** in your body to make them move.

If there were no forces to pull and push, everything would stay still. Imagine how quiet the world would be!

Moving along

Cars and bicycles only move when a force pushes them along. When the force stops, they slow down and stop.

Pushing force from the muscles in your legs presses the bicycle pedals. The pedals turn the wheels and the wheels roll the bicycle along.

A train has a powerful **engine** that makes a large amount of **energy**. The train uses this energy to pull its carriages.

Train carriages cannot move along by themselves. They need the engine to pull them.

It is hard work to pedal a bike uphill. This is because a force called **gravity** is pulling downhill at the same time.

Stop and change direction

When you throw, kick or hit a ball hard, it flies fast through the air. If you use less force, the ball will not go as fast or as far.

When you hit a tennis ball it goes a long way.

When a moving ball hits something hard, like the ground, it will bounce and change **direction**. If it hits something soft, like a net, it will slow down and stop.

When your friend hits the ball back, he makes it change direction.

When you catch the ball, you stop it moving.

Friction

When two things rub together they make a force called **friction**. Friction slows things down and makes them stop.

Ice skaters can speed along because ice skates are smooth. They don't make much friction as they slip easily over the ice.

Two smooth surfaces rubbing together make less friction than two rough surfaces rubbing together.

The patterned, rough soles on snow boots grip the ground.
They help to stop you slipping and falling over.

Brake blocks press against the rim of the wheel of a vehicle. This makes friction, which slows the wheel down.

Moving through air and water

Air and water slow everything down that tries to move through them. This happens because of forces called **air and water resistance**.

The shape of an aeroplane is "**streamlined**". This shape helps it to cut through the air.

A shark moves
its tail from side to side to
push it along.

Water is thicker than air. This makes
it harder work for you to run through
water than it is to run through air.

Water rubs against a shark as it swims. It has a
pointed body for speeding through the water.

Twist and turn

All kinds of things you use every day need a twist or a turn to make them move. You grip a jar with one hand and twist the lid to take it off with the other hand.

Your muscles give you the strength to twist off the lid and put it back on again.

Some jobs are hard to do just using your own hands. Tools and handles can help you to twist and turn with extra force.

A screwdriver helps you to twist and untwist screws.

You turn a door knob to open a door. You twist a tap to turn on the water. You twist a spanner to turn nuts and bolts.

Squash and stretch

You can squash and stretch some materials into different shapes. They will keep their new shape until you squash or stretch them again.

You can make all kinds of new shapes by squashing and stretching modelling clay.

A balloon is made of rubber. The rubber stretches and gets bigger when you fill it with air.

Blowing too much air into a balloon can stretch it so much that it pops.

Rubber is a form of **elastic**. It stretches when you pull it. When you let it go it snaps back with an elastic force called **tension**.

When the air escapes, the balloon springs back and becomes small again.

Falling down

Whenever you jump up in the air, you always fall back down. This happens because of a force called gravity.

Gravity pulls everything down to the ground.

If there was no gravity pulling downwards, everything on **Earth** would float off into **space**.

A parachute lets you fall slowly through the air and gives you a soft landing.

Gravity pulls a parachute down to the ground. At the same time, air pushes up on the parachute and this helps it **float** down slowly.

Heavy and light

Weight is gravity pulling on objects. A heavy object, such as a bag full of shopping, is hard to lift because as you pull up the bag, gravity is pulling it down.

A balloon is quite big but it is light. This is because it is full of air.

A tin of cat food is smaller than a balloon, but it is heavier. This is because the can is full of heavy food.

Big things can feel lighter than things that are much smaller. A pillow, for example, is lighter to carry than a brick.

Floating and sinking

The force of gravity pulls things down in the water. At the same time, water pushes them up with a force called **upthrust**. Things float or **sink** because of their shape, size and the material that they are made of.

A pebble is small but it sinks because it is heavy for its size. Upthrust is not strong enough to keep it afloat.

A beach ball is bigger than a pebble. It floats because it is light and full of air.

A big boat floats because it has spaces inside it that are full of air, so it is light for its size.

Things will float when they are light for their size, because the force of upthrust can hold them up in the water.

Magnets

A magnet is a piece of metal that has a natural force called **magnetism**. It pulls things made of iron or steel towards it.

A magnet doesn't pick up things made of plastic, paper and wood.

In places where there are no signposts, a **compass** helps you to find the way.

A compass needle is a magnet. It always points to the north, so you know in which direction you are facing.

If you hang a bar magnet on a thread, one end will swing to face north and the other end will face south.

Wind and waves

Wind and waves are natural forces that push against things and make them move. You can feel wind pushing against you. It moves your clothes and hair.

Wind is moving air. It pushes against the sails of a yacht and speeds it along.

The surfer rides along on the force of a big wave.

Wind blows over the sea and makes ripples and waves. A strong wind makes big waves.

MAKE A PARACHUTE

Make a parachute that floats down to the ground.

YOU WILL NEED:

- a square of tissue paper 20 cm by 20 cm
- 4 pieces of cotton thread 15 cm long
- sticky tape
- 2 paper clips

1 Stick a thread to each corner of the tissue paper square.

2 Tie the four ends of thread together in a knot.

3 Hang the two paperclips from the knot.

4 Stand on a chair (be careful) and throw the parachute in the air. Watch it float down.

Air pushes up against the parachute at the same time as gravity pulls it down to the ground.

Words to remember

air resistance The way air pushes against things that move through it and slows them down.

bones The frame of your body, the skeleton, is made up of bones joined together.

brake Slows down and stops things that move, such as bicycles and cars.

compass A machine to help you to find your way. It has a needle, which is a magnet. The needle always points to the north.

direction The way something is pointing or moving. Left and right are directions. North, south, east and west are directions that help us to find our way.

Earth A ball of rock in space. It is the planet we live on.

elastic Something that can be stretched and springs back again when it is let go, such as a balloon.

energy Gives people and machines the power they need to work. Nothing can work without energy.

engine Gives a machine the power to work. A washing machine engine uses electricity and a car engine burns petrol to work.

float Does not sink to the bottom or down to the ground. A boat floats on the water. A hot air balloon floats in the air.

force A push or a pull. It makes something move, go faster, slow down or stop.

friction A force made when two things rub together. For example, a book rubbing against a table or an aeroplane flying through the air.

gravity A force that pulls everything towards the ground. It makes things you drop fall down.

magnetism A force that pulls things made of iron and steel towards a magnet.

muscles Are attached to your bones. They pull your bones and let you move.

sinks Does not float in the water or in the air. A pebble sinks under water. A parachute sinks slowly to the ground.

space The planets, stars and galaxies beyond the Earth.

streamlined A smooth and pointed shape, which helps things to move easily through air and water, such as an aeroplane or speedboat.

tension A kind of force. When you stretch elastic or press down on a spring, you can feel the force of tension.

upthrust The force made by water pushing up on things that float.

water resistance The way water pushes against things that move through it and slows them down.

weight Gravity pulling down on something gives it weight. We can measure how much something weighs with scales.

Index

aeroplane 12

air 12–13, 17, 18, 19, 20, 23, 26

balloon 17, 20–21

bones 5

brake 11

compass 25

direction 8–9, 25

Earth 19

elastic 17

energy 7

engine 7

float 19, 22–23

forces 4–5, 6–7, 8, 10, 12, 15, 17, 18, 22–23, 26, 27

friction 10–11

gravity 7, 18–19, 20, 22

heavy 20, 21, 22

light 20, 21, 23

magnet 24–25

muscles 5, 6, 14

parachute 19, 28

shark 13

sink 22

slow down 6, 9, 10, 11, 12

squash 16

stop 6, 9,10

streamlined shape 12–13

stretch 16–17

tension 17

turn 14–15

twist 14–15

upthrust 22–23

wave 26–27

weight 20

wind 26–27